Phyllida Barlow

STINT

Published on the occasion of the exhibition

Phyllida Barlow STINT

Curated by Ronnie Simpson
Organised by the Mead Gallery
4 October — 6 December 2008

Mead Gallery
Warwick Arts Centre,
University of Warwick
Coventry CV4 7AL
T +44 (0)24 7652 4524
www.warwickartscentre.co.uk

Louise Adams—Visitor Services Co-ordinator
Liz Dooley—Curatorial Assistant
Ella Elphick—Gallery Assistant
David Garnett—Technician, assisted by Tom Barker,
Mark Davey, Brian McStay, Nick Mortimer,
Steve Shiell, Michael Vaughan, Charlie Yetton
Mel Lloyd-Smith—Curatorial Associate
Amanda McDonnell—Gallery Assistant
Rebecca Richards—Gallery Assistant
Irene Rickhuss—Gallery Assistant
Sarah Shalgosky—Curator
Ronnie Simpson—Exhibitions Director

Catalogue copyright ©2008 Mead Gallery
Text copyright ©Mead Gallery
Images copyright ©Phyllida Barlow
Photography by Fabian Peake and Francis Ware

Published in an edition of 500 by Mead Gallery,
The University of Warwick.

Edited by Ronnie Simpson
Designed by Stefi Orazi
Printed and bound in England by Xtraprint Limited

Distributed by Cornerhouse Publications
70 Oxford Street, Manchester M1 5NH
T +44 (0)161 200 1503 F +44 (0)161 200 1505
www.cornerhouse.org

ISBN 978-0-902683-89-1

Between a stroke and a smack

Phyllida Barlow in conversation with Ronnie Simpson

RONNIE SIMPSON STINT picks up from your Black Dog publication, *Objects For...and Other Things*, and your 2004 exhibition, 'Peninsula' at BALTIC, Gateshead.

Can you tell me what you aim to achieve with STINT?

PHYLLIDA BARLOW STINT for me is an important opportunity to carry on some of the things that happened in the BALTIC exhibition.

The BALTIC piece was very much about taking the processes of making to some sort of physical edge—where things were going to be out of reach—completely beyond a certain physical span, both horizontally, vertically and diagonally. There were going to be things happening where weight would balance something or crush something, so everything was going to be married to a kind of gesture. A physical gesture, but on a size and a scale that I hadn't been able to really do before, in quite that kind of space, or in quite that well-funded way. So it was a real adventure. And I see the Mead Gallery offering the same possibilities.

And you're revisiting some of the works from the BALTIC, such as the Barrier piece, which will be a new version of that work for Mead.

There were pieces in the BALTIC exhibition that physically needed another level of endeavour. We had all been involved in this intense performative process making the Barrier, but the final work was disappointing. Barrier was meant to chop the gallery up, but it wasn't high enough, and merely titillated the space. The piece needed to be twice the height and not so regimented. It was over-planned and over-delivered, and needed an axe taken to it.

In more general terms, what are you aiming to achieve when you revisit and remake works?

It's always about upping some aspect of it. It's easy to say of somebody's work, 'It's too this, it's too neat and tidy, it needs roughing up, it needs duffing down'. But that might not be the way someone like me wants to go. I don't just want to build something and take an axe to it. I've done that and it's as formulaic as any other gesture. It's something much more controlled that I want to do.

Therefore, the revisiting of it will be quite specific. Like playing on that double edge of fear and pleasure. Or the deceit of something looking decorative, but also being quite brutal. So those qualities are really important in trying to make those elements even more poignant or tough.

BETWEEN A STROKE AND A SMACK

Peninsula
———
BALTIC
Centre for Contemporary Art,
Gateshead
2004–2005

Timber lengths, paint, painted
hardboard, tape, paper, Formica,
fabric, rubber, rope, plastic
tube, concrete, polystyrene,
felt, upholstery foam, cardboard
Dimensions: Variable

Inherent in the title is a sense of reluctance, of having to do your STINT?

STINT I see as an endurance. There's a level of endurance in preparing for something like the Barrier piece which will go across the Mead space. The work reflects the barrier from BALTIC, but it will be a much more skeletal, and I hope, more playful, intervention in the space. It will require a tremendous physical commitment to realise the work, and that will require me to be very clear headed in setting it up and directing people on what to do. STINT is about a level of endurance that takes both a mental and a physical process to somewhere, but I'm not quite sure what that is.

Despite their large scale, the works somehow manage to retain a sense of intimacy.

These large exhibitions, where I'm making big pieces, sometimes undermine a more private, intimate love of making. It puts it into a different realm. But when it comes to something as close to the work as wrapping tape around it, then I think something returns. I'm able to say, 'No, let's put the reds there and the blacks there.' It becomes very painterly. As though I can move back again very fluidly across the piece on that sort of scale. But it's not like holding something in my hand and being able to resolve what I want to do on that kind of smaller scale.

The most important thing about these big exhibitions is to retain something of what happens in the studio within the exhibition. That it's not just a factory. That something of the intimacy of the studio process is still retained within the finished works that end up in the exhibition. So it's still there, but it's taking another form.

Is violence important in the work?

Yes, it is actually. The idea, which I think Louise Bourgeois talks about very well, that the actions of making are often associated with quite violent gestures—chopping, cutting etc. When you transfer them to making sculpture they're very legitimate. And they're not legitimate if you're not applying them in that kind of way. And the urgency to get something done is very important in my work. I make work very quickly. I then need ages to understand what I've done, and that is an odd paradox. I've talked to a lot of other people who make work very quickly, and they almost don't know what they've done. They don't know where it's come from. And that's quite bewildering. You've put everything into the work, and you look at the thing and you haven't got a clue what it is. I haven't got a clue what it is.

Or how it'll be received?

Exactly, absolutely! You don't know where it sits in any kind of critical spectrum. You're left with this very raw thing. Sometimes that sort of work can look as though it's a mannerism of some sort. But it isn't. It's what's been possible in that time, at that particular point. If it was made half an hour later it would be different. All these things have to be taken into consideration with that way of working.

You then need this inordinate amount of time to work out what the next thing is going to be, or what that thing is that you've just done. And I still find that very disconcerting. Making things very big prolongs that action and enables one to have a more contemplative relationship with the work.

And when I say I don't know what the subject is, I really don't. Therefore there is an ongoing chase to find that. I sort of know what the content is. And I can know what the form is—like the Barrier, or a heap of crushed stuff, or objects that look as if they might have just fallen over. But what the subject within that is, I don't know.

Does that become clearer over time?

No. The subject has often been what the objects are doing. It's a very active thing.

Say I look at a piece of my work from 1967/1968 and it's using a certain paint—it really touches a chord. It makes me realise that there's been an absolute consistent obsession with the duality of surfaces. The surface of the actual thing, and the surface of something that's imposed over it. That is to do with that first relationship with clay, when it comes in this fantastic raw lump and you give it a whack and it's taken the imprint of that action absolutely like magic.

And for some people who maybe get into art, and they are being driven the whole time through getting it right or observation, to suddenly be given a completely new way of being an artist and recognising how you might transfer that visual thing into something else—a physical action—is a real epiphany. And it certainly happened to me.

That way of working, of maintaining the creative aspect while you're making the work in the space, is quite a traditional position isn't it?

Oh God, yes!

One of the few places it still exists is in the use of the readymade, where a spontaneous act of improvisation shifts ones perception

Untitled 2:

`timber, tape, painted hardboard;`

`2008`

Kilkenny Arts Festival,
Rothe House, Kilkenny, Ireland

Dimensions: Variable

and there's a significant transformation. In the opposite way to the made-easy object which you've referred to in the past.

Totally, absolutely! That's what I've found very surprising over the last couple of decades. Maybe what I saw as a very normal way of working—having tested things out in the studio, then to go to a site with various materials where you would then repeat that rehearsal for real in the space—how that way of working has seemed unusual, when I don't think it is. I think you're absolutely right—it's very traditional. Is it because we live in such an object-based art world, with the prevalence of the commodifiable art object, that somebody who improvises on the spot is now considered high-risk?

And there are lots of artists who are working in that way all round the world. Making work in situ, and impermanence, do seem to stand in opposition to commodification. Impermanence does not have to be non-commercial, and it isn't. Works can be replenished, or have an after-life in some other form. Imperpetuity is an impossibility in any material, including bronze and stone. And I am not interested in imperpetuity for its own sake. I'm interested in some kind of life cycle—an existence with a beginning, middle, and end. My way of making work is traditional. But it's not always about an end result, although that is important. And it's not as if my work is made out of ice or something.

How does paint work in the sculpture for you?

It's like an act of resolution. It finishes it. And I've always seen paint as that. I've seen it very much like clay. Clay is inherently within everything I do. The act of being able to build something up with a material that, if it's not kept damp, is going to dry out and solidify. And then it finalises something. It has its own control inherent within it. I think something about paint has that quality too—that it's going to dry, and then seal the surface. And that's almost a kind of reminder that the work won't have anything more done to it.

Tape is the same—these differently coloured tapes I use. There's an act of wrapping that goes on with tape, and an act of folding and smothering with clay, that's both like trying to find a moment to finish that isn't necessarily ever particularly clear. There could be another layer of paint, or there could be another layer of tape put on. It could go on and on forever. But it doesn't.

Those kinds of verbs are important to you—wrapping, folding, smothering...

There are other issues that have come into play which I'd be interested to

know how they can evolve a critical language that is favourable to them. The idea of theatricality and largeness, and what those things are. They can be condemned as self-indulgent. And I don't see them as that. I see them as more like a giving-out than withdrawing-from. I don't quite know what the act of looking is sometimes with very large works like a Richard Serra. Is there another experience that's actually going on that's almost apart from the visual? Is it about just an overall sensation rather than only a visual sensation?

What is the attraction to working on that scale? What are you trying to articulate through largeness?

In hindsight I can say, because I make work so quickly somehow the largeness is a way of challenging that. It enables something to be slowed down a bit and gives me a chance to examine what I'm doing physically. But also it has a lot to do with what I'm physically capable of.

Which you've always challenged?

Yes. What I like about large sculpture is that sense of your own physicality and its relationship to it. And that this thing isn't a ship or a building, it's this artifice object that's making us think about things like scale and physicality. There's something about walking around sculpture that has the possibility to be reflective, like walking through a landscape. There are lots of things which size and scale can be compared to—a sculpture isn't those things, but it can take us there. And I think the largeness of sculpture has that infinite possibility to make one engage beyond just the object itself, and into other realms of experience. Again, very different from the pictorial experience of looking at and into a painting, which is much more cerebral.

You described it well previously: *'For me, the structures are like the land, and the stuff that gets flung on them is anything that isn't land: weather, emotions, mess, memories...'* How people bring themselves and their lives to the experience of the work. Is that what you mean by the theatricality of the work—the 'suspension of disbelief' you're interested in?

There's something about my wanting to not belie. I want the fact that it's the cheapest 2"×1" timber, or the cheapest hardboard you can get, to be blatant and disclosed. I want those materials to be untransformed. Therefore, what the transformative experience is, I'm very unclear about. And in that unclearness there is also a subject I'm not clear about. So the 'suspension of disbelief' and its relation to the 'suspension of belief' seems to be on a knife edge.

BETWEEN A STROKE AND A SMACK

Untitled:
__hardboard, timber, felt, paint,__
__plaster; 2007__
From 'Etc.',
Amagerfaelledvej Art Project,
Copenhagen, Denmark
Dimensions: Variable

The materials are what they are, but they're acting out a fantasy— offering an absurd possibility of being?

We know when we look at the stage, that it's a stage. Nothing is going to change our mind about that, because that is why we've gone to the theatre. And that's the joy of the gallery. We know it's an art gallery, and that's why it's such a different experience from using public space where an intervention then has to separate itself from that, and that's very interesting. But it's a very different experience in terms of what you're trying to convince people they are looking at.

For myself, when making work for a gallery, 50 percent of the work is done for you. The gallery is like a stage. Then what are these people that come in to see it? What is the audience? And to me they are on an absolute par with the thing they are looking at. The work and the viewers are all protagonists. There isn't a hierarchy between viewer and object. The viewer would be invited to walk, wander, look up, down, through. They are engaging with the work as an equal partner. The work itself would be inviting them to behave in a certain way.

Obviously they don't have to, or they may not, but it's not as though the work is an entirely passive commodity that's got to be read or interpreted through a verbal language based experience. That will come into it, but I hope the physicality between viewer and object is very shared— is communal. It's that aspect of a sculptural language that I'm still interested in.

The works can be comparable more to things like obstacles or interruptions. In that sense they have characteristics like aggression, or overwhelmingness, or absurdity. Things that aren't just visual, but are sensations of physicality.

I'm not interested in the audience seeing wood as bones. I'm not interested in that narrative transformation. I'm much more interested in them recognising an action, and that the action maybe is quite illogical. And the action is over quite a big expanse, or is compressed and crushed, like some of the pieces I'll be doing at the Mead.

The paint is often a kind of artifice. It looks as though it's pretending to be something, but it isn't, it's just paint. And the big black piece I'll be doing for the Mead will be very, very theatrical. It already looks like charred, burnt remains. But it's not—it's just paint. I enjoy that edge that things might remind one of, but actually in the end it is what it is. It's paint and fabric and polystyrene. It's not the remains of a burnt out nightclub or something.

8

What are the elements that make theatre?

A relationship with a thing that isn't yourself. Artifice to which you are a witness. I was speaking on Friday in Scotland about that phrase 'the suspension of disbelief', and my lack of understanding about it in relation to the phrase 'suspension of belief'. What is the difference between the two?

There was a young chap there who was a theatre person and he was intrigued by that, and was saying it was all about rules. And I said, 'Yes. In the theatre, when Hamlet goes into that state of despair you don't leap onto the stage and try to comfort him. And is that what that belief/disbelief thing is about?' You're sitting in the theatre and you're looking at this thing. You believe it because you have suspended disbelief in order to believe it. Then if you suspend your belief, you're no longer believing in what you're looking at. So you go round and round in circles. And that to me is very much like looking at a sculpture. More with things that occupy the same space as us— real space—than with a painting where there's a kind of dream state you can go into.

The 'suspension of belief' would seem more related to narrative, and the 'suspension of disbelief' to the unconscious? Does the stage provide a space for the unconscious?

I would deeply hope so. A whole other layer of seeing that is not visual. It could even be to do with boredom, or not being interested for a moment, and all sorts of things that happen when you're expected to concentrate and your mind is constantly wandering, sliding over what you're meant to be engaging with. I'm very interested in that experience of being in a place or a time where there is an expectation to be utterly engaged, and yet, for most people there is a kind of drifting. It's like listening to poetry being read out loud, or being at a concert. Are you 100 percent engaged 100 percent of the time? What happens in those lapses?

I remember Cornelia Parker's piece at the Tate, where she draped a mile of string around a Rodin sculpture, 'The Kiss'. I thought it was fascinating the way the string became like a hand caressing the work. It was demonstrating a tactile experience without the viewer having to literally touch the work. It took me into this state of reverie. One might have been looking at the string moving over an arm, then onto the thigh, and up the side of the rib cage, or whatever it was doing. But I was thinking about something completely different, and yet absolutely involved in looking at that work. I think I was thinking about the process of touch. I can recall it very vividly, that process of actually being there. There is a state of 'being in the presence of'—which isn't about being totally engaged in a fully observant

Untitled:

ramp, tower, flags; 2007

Festival Internacional de Arte,
Galeria Jesus Gallardo,
Leon, Mexico

Painted board, painted timber,
plaster board, rope, fabric,
paper, tape
Dimensions: 18 m × 6 m × 12 m

way—that is interesting in terms of looking at, and walking around, sculpture. And that's where belief/disbelief comes into play.

And maybe I'm talking about belief in a way that when you see something and you know what it's made of, or you know how it's done, or it reveals itself—it discloses itself in all its rawness—then what is the other side of that? What is the flip side—that isn't just demonstrating that, but is doing something else as well? I see the belief/disbelief thing as oscillating on that edge—knowing and being there with it, and maybe a kind of time factor in how you are engaging with it.

That links to your studio practice—the scenario where the creative process becomes quite unconscious.

With these big shows the delegation of tasks to assistants ratchets up the whole experience of making to another level. I now realise that the process of setting up in the space is when I reclaim a lot of what I was not able to do in the studio. And that becomes very exciting and dynamic. The Heap piece at the Mead—all the black stuff—because we couldn't test it all out properly beforehand, we only know the bare essentials about that work. It's going to be a big revelatory process of what that's going to become as a work in the gallery. And I hope that will give the work a sense of urgency.

A question which also relates to the theatrical element—when do you know a sculpture isn't for being climbed all over? The thing people say to me the whole time is that they long to touch my work. But I don't want people to touch my work. I hate that! I hate that interaction. But the longing to touch it is quite an interesting area to get into. Wanting to touch is an action that is being withheld. Tactility requires imagination when the act of touching cannot be fulfilled. Imagining the sensation of touch is a language—a very non-verbal language.

'The longing to touch' is interesting, because your work does engender a sense of wanting to hold these things in some way. Why do you think there is that longing?

Using mundane materials like tape, ready-to-go timber lengths, and familiar fabrics, like felt, have a domestic connotation. Tape is used in a very hands-on way. It's an everyday material in use in the home, the office, and industry. If it's used on an artwork it sets up a tension about familiarity in that everyday sense, and familiarity of touch which immediately makes people want to reach out and do that.

Going back to the Cornelia Parker string piece—the fact that the string was doing the touching became so intriguing. Just as imagining what it is like to touch—that is such a powerful language in itself. Through the popularising of art, it has been seen as a kind of right of the viewer that they are allowed to touch. That they're given the opportunity to do it, rather than it being seen more in terms of theatre and performance, or even with paintings, where it is absolutely not okay to touch.

I think there's been a confusion how an audience responds to the visual arts. This notion that it's all fun and can be picked up and thrown around the room, I find it excruciating. Whereas, it is provocative, unresolved and open-ended to prompt a thinking process, or a dreaming and imaginative process, that says, 'Well, what are these surfaces like?' I want to be the last person who has touched the work—not the viewer.

The materials you use could be described as functional, ugly, ubiquitous. Why those materials?

Because they are so accessible. They're manufactured to be used in a specific way in terms of the building trade.

To go on about the theatrical... In order to retain that sense of intimacy that the studio can offer, the processes of installing a show become a surrogate version of that intimacy, where the installing process is a kind of acting out, a re-making, often in a drastic way, as well as from scratch, of what had been prepared, rehearsed, in the studio. What I hope to deliver in the work is the experience of actually being in the activity of the work itself. And if it can't be remembered after the event, I'm not too bothered about that. Because maybe some of those words you were saying were important to me, perhaps they might be remembered. Rather than an exact, precise image being recalled, it might be the felt fabric being thrown over a heap of polystyrene, or a mass of crushed things. And that they present a state of mind and a state of consciousness in that time of being in the presence of the work. Perhaps that's what gets retained, or I would hope that's what is retained.

Maybe that is comparable to the experience of listening to music. What are you actually experiencing? When the event is over, how do you recall that? It can seem in complete contrast to the sort of absurd vastness of an orchestra or whatever the event is. You're at the end of all that, you're almost left with nothing.

I see the paradox of what I do being similar to that. The endeavour, all that time spent pulling tape or fixing timbers, struts, or whatever. And actually, the qualities that may get remembered are to do with looking up, looking across, looking through and into, walking around. That's where I see the theatrical. Not as a suspension of disbelief, but as an active experience

BETWEEN A STROKE AND A SMACK

Untitled × 2:

hardboard, rubber, tape, fabric,

timber, plaster, paint; 2006

From 'Beauty and the Beast',
Fieldgate Gallery,
Whitechapel, London
2006

Dimensions: Variable

where the physical act of looking at the work—looking up across etc, and walking around the works and the space—that this physical engagement will see things for what they are.

What you seem to be describing is the process of putting on a show—whether it's art, music, theatre—that there's a strange interrelation between the perfunctory and the creative processes. In your work both are evident. The method of construction and use of untransformed materials are married to the creative process and sense of intimacy in their conception and construction.

It would be great if the work occasionally managed to offer an abbreviated way of existing, but managed to provide something that also lasted. Which I suppose is what performance does in its own extraordinarily contradictory way. You go there for three hours and you come away—and it's difficult to know what you come away with, other than a mood that's been generated and prompted by the thing you've just been to—which may have been a huge event of every single technical thing possible to get it launched. What you go away with is something utterly intangible.

To be making these huge things that require these vast quantities of materials, and actions of binding and wrapping, for something that is the absolute opposite of that, does beg a lot of questions. It makes me think a lot about the politics of making art, and the politics of generating a mood. And is a mood a political thing? Does it tie in with something that has bigger issues to do with how we can live in environments that are highly managed? Decisions are taken without us knowing how those motorways got built, or how those barriers got put there, or that huge building complex is suddenly going up. We have no means for knowing how to intervene on those things. Therefore what they're doing to us is creating a kind of state of mind. It does seem to me there is a political link there—about the physicality of the world we live in and what it generates in terms of something that is extraordinarily potent but utterly invisible. I think that's quite an important aspect of something to do with the visual arts.

There's a fantastic photograph of Guantanamo Bay that had a huge impact on me in terms of the Barrier I'm doing at the Mead. It was a photo of these tiny bits of orange thread which the inmates had pulled from their suits and wound round the metal steel fencing. I don't know what the orange thread was meant to convey, its message, or what it said, or what its significance was—but the beauty of it, the decorativeness of it, combined with knowing about the horrific circumstances of that place, is extraordinarily potent and contradictory.

It's not just the image—it's also that the thread somehow takes you into the minds of those inmates. It's a sign of some sort that is completely against the harshness of that ghastly environment. Again, it's that kind of opposite way of something being in the world—that it's something incredibly permanent and ferocious, which is then simultaneously changed into something ephemeral and delicate.

Can you tell us more about the materials?

Clay was such a liberating material when I first started making sculpture. Wanting the clay to become more and more—literally. And realising I couldn't. I needed all sorts of things to make clay work on a really big scale. That was when I started to use huge quantities of found, discarded materials—paper, all sorts of stuff found in skips.

One thing which was important was that it could be crushable in some way, malleable. And that the wood, metal, timber components were there just as props to being able to condense and compress these crushable materials. To be rough and brutal—to be physical.

Then getting rid of that idea altogether for a time—not wanting to use second-hand materials, wanting to use absolutely pristine new materials, but still wanting to make these pristine materials perform in that kind of way. And without any kind of support—to make the materials, and their processes, self-supporting. Then the 'structural' components became things in themselves, liberated from these crushed materials.

The resources for materials that could have that done to them, that amount of physical engagement, were builders merchants where you could see huge stacks of things like insulating board, hardboard, cheap timber, asphaltic roofing felt, polythene, as well as materials that you can use very directly, like plaster. And it can hold things in place, fossilise things, trap things. That's the history of those materials. And certainly not trying to camouflage them, but make them take on a physical presence through the way they were being pushed, pulled, stretched, balanced, singled-out, etc. So that the transformation is much more within the action than trying to say this is polystyrene pretending to be whatever. I'm not interested in that.

The paint often does play that sort of game as a kind of cosmetic veneer over the surface. But then I want to get the two working together. I want the skins of paint to be seen, but also the edges of the material it's over. I'm trying to show the way things do get covered and hidden. And looking at something like nostalgia comes into that. The contradiction of something being very instant and new, but looking quite damaged and ruined is another aspect of paradox and theatricality.

Expediency seems an important factor in your choice of materials and the way you work.

It's incredibly important. It has a huge control on trying out new things. The BALTIC was a landmark of testing out sheer size and breadth and weight, and all that kind of thing. I was using expedient materials like polystyrene, assembling long timber lengths in sections, and relying on materials and construction methods which lent themselves to being very simply and quickly assembled. And using concrete to make the bollards that held the long posts up—using everyday solutions culled from road works, and quick-fix methods used domestically to resolve problems of size, scale and weight. I wasn't interested in trying to find yet another material that would do that.

Expediency and endeavour...

There are things about endeavour, expediency and endurance that are a really important subject in the work. And maybe with that goes the word entropy. I see there's something about fatigue in that word, possibly a kind of fatigue that's very much in the present tense. It's not like looking at something that's exhausted. It's almost like the fatigue is about an arrival, rather than it being retrospective. There are some of these materials that still have the potential to use that. I'm hoping that the Barrier and the Heap piece I'm doing for Mead will have something of that about them.

← black painted pom poms.

Heap

concret
+
wire netting
lumps

stack.

Barrier

Hoardings

crushed box

ramp.

Tubs

signs

2   fallen props

SKIT

Bloomberg Space,
Finsbury Square, London
2005

Timber, paper, fabrics, plastic,
card, newspaper, rubber, paint,
hardboard, plastic tube, board
Dimensions: Variable

something else. And that is why I am trying to look at the experience of
making these things, and the sense of timing of that experience and what
that was—and was it very much about the now of it?

When you're making new works you're bringing that back?

Yes, and also trying to challenge that. In this exhibition at the Mead, what
I'm trying to challenge is something about the use of colour. Bringing into
the show these very raw, half-finished components that will bounce off the
big coloured elements. There will be works that reveal the state before this
habitual finishing through paint. Maybe I'm trying to question what that
paint thing is about by not doing it. Leaving some of the works in their raw
state feels quite edgy.

**The element of rawness is always evident in your work.
The hardness and duplicity of the materials creating these
absurd objects and gestures.**

Yes. Trying to do two things that are quite opposite. One is to not play any
tricks with what the materials are. But, on the other hand, to play
loads of tricks making these—'absurd objects'. And I hope they are absurd,
because they're pointless. But that is what often causes me frustration.
I don't know what their meaning is, or how important that is anyway—
especially in that very deconstructive way of being able to trace them
back to a system of readings and interpretations that all dovetail and
lock together. I don't think there is that in the work. Nor do I want it to be
in the work.

Which is what makes the works so alive?

But I think it is on a knife-edge. It can flip. It can shoot itself in the foot.
Therefore, how it plays those two things is absolutely crucial. And I'm
beginning to feel that the over-layering of the paint is becoming an
affectation that needs to be challenged. As a visual ploy it isn't doing what
it did originally—which was to create this absurd cosmetic surface. It
wasn't necessary. It was an absurd act. And I'm just beginning to wonder
whether it isn't becoming too much of a trademark—less about finding a
way of going back again to previous more irrational, material ways of using
paint, not just for its colour and surface. Which I would like to do—to use
paint in more than just a visual way. Before, it was also doing other things,
which was how I first started to use it years ago, using paint as part of
the construction and making process so that it held the surfaces together,
like clay and plaster.

And the absurd object offers a stage for the viewer's unconscious?

My ideal viewer would be somebody who would be enjoying being flummoxed by the work. They can see something is blocking off the space, but there is no reason for it to be blocked off. So there is almost a playful sense of bringing into a very controlled space like a gallery familiar devices that we've experienced in our everyday life, which are then heightened to a point of absolute absurdity.

So there's a Barrier that's built absolutely like a barrier, but is also very decorative. I would hope that a viewer might on the one hand see it as playful—almost festive—like something you get at a big festival concert. But at the same time slightly threatening, and reminiscent of ways that forbid and control, and how these two states of existence are so close to each other. Like the difference between a stroke and a smack, or a caress and a punch.

Throughout your career you've constantly made great efforts to maintain a critical forum for the discussion of issues relevant to contemporary sculpture. This has been problematic in that there are now all these myths attached to your work and your position as an artist.

If you get on your hobbyhorse and shout and rant and roar about it, you're actually also shooting yourself in the foot. I've done that a bit in protesting too much about the demise of sculpture, then realising that actually I couldn't care less, and that there's too much going on that's interesting to rant and roar about something that doesn't need to claim a language in that specific sense that I was beginning to demand.

Did that come from your position as an artist or as an educator?

I think it came from my position very much as an artist, and a fear that I wasn't going to have anything of interest to offer as an educator. Because a kind of language was disappearing—and then realising that was absurd. It wasn't disappearing. It was transforming in a million and one different ways.

The language of the visual arts has evolved in so many disparate ways. People are making sculptural things without knowing a great deal about sculpture at all. They're not coming through those disciplines of sculpture, say casting or constructing, or through the radical gestures of the 60s and 70s—Smithson and Matta Clark, for example—but they're finding ways of using space that are incredibly exciting. Take someone like Thomas Hirschorn, or Torres, who are doing things, but are not announcing themselves as sculptors. It is the work itself that counts, first and foremost.

But wasn't that also a language you were challenging?

Untitled ×9:

Timber, plywood, felt, paper,

cardboard, rubber, plaster,

concrete, tape, paint

From the commission 'Underover',
1 Canada Square,
Canary Wharf, London
2008

Dimensions: Variable

Very—but that was what I was beginning to forget. And it took someone to remind me about all those works where I wasn't using inside structures to objects. I'd abandoned the armature and made the work in situ very theatrically. That was all a huge challenge to sculptural language in that orthodox way. When I was trying to develop an argument which was asking, 'Does sculpture have a language?', I was forgetting what my own history was saying. I created an intellectual problem for myself:

1. What did I mean by sculpture?

2. What was my relationship with the work I'd done in the past which seemed to really challenge this?

and

3. What was my relationship with these big physical things I seem to be making now? Were they meant to be like a born-again sculpture type thing? Absolutely not, no!

Courage is an incredibly important thing. Having the courage to say absolutely what you're feeling at a particular time. Also, knowing that that can get one—and has got me—into a lot of trouble. One starts representing what seems like idealistic positions when I'm not interested in idealistic positions. I'm just interested in how we keep a critical discussion going about making art in a time when there are huge market-driven forces at work which tend to breed a complacency about critical discussion. If something is successful financially in terms of buying and selling, the critical discourse that builds up around it has to take that into consideration, and that seems quite problematic. The economic value of an art work seems to stall its critical dynamic.

The pursuit of a critical discourse remains hugely important to you?

Yes. When I was talking to Mark Godfrey in the 'Objects for...' monograph he said, 'You go on too much about sculpture.' That made me realise that what I was referring to was so historical. And, at a stroke, I just did not want to be locked into that historicism.

I've been so passionately interested in how people make work now. Whether it's called sculpture or not isn't actually that important. And I don't think I would have been able to have worked with so many young artists, as I have done and continue to do, if I had doggedly been the kind of academic saying, 'Well it's not like a Bruce Nauman or Robert Smithson.' Those artists are historical monuments who did things at a particular time. Emulating them can be pointless. However, it is interesting how somebody would do those things now. Of course loads of people have reinvented and replayed those historical moments, sometimes without even knowing about those artists.

Critically, I don't know how you then join up those dots, or whether one should bother to, or what all our roles are in this. I think it's really important people know about these people and points in history—Boetti, Pistoletto, Broodthaers, Hesse, Smithson, Matta Clark—all these artists who were using these kind of materials and gestures way back 30 or 40 years ago.

But without that knowledge, strong work can still be made. What does that say? That's the kind of critical discourse I'm interested in. There is a lot of art that can be made without that historical baggage. Therefore, to be constantly playing the 60s/70s record needs to be challenged. Young artists have the right to say, 'Art begins today.' To claim that position, even though it comes with a lot of risks.

What I didn't want was finding that my passion for a certain kind of sculpture prohibited me from doing what I really love doing—making work and then looking at work—especially the work of young artists. I was having to obey a set of rules of my own invention, which demanded evidence of my passion for sculpture. No, I didn't want those rules, or that control or belief system.

In 20 years the whole market has changed dramatically.

Yes, it underpins how people come into the art world, and how artists with a long history of making exist in the art world now. It's altered everything, and one would have to be very naïve, or extremely rich, to be able to ignore it.

There are lots of forces at play that constantly make one question what one's role is as an artist. Therefore, if you take on a very vehement, passionate position, that position has to be contextualised within an art world that has very powerful motives. It is an art world that is driven by all sorts of forces, many of which might be completely at odds with those passionate concerns. I think that a lot of artists find themselves in that position. And possibly then get slightly wrong-footed by that. By having passion!

And has your role as an artist changed with that?

I emerged into the art world in the sixties. There was a very changed metabolism going on then with the New Generation shows at the Whitechapel. Young artists were being profiled in quite dynamic ways compared with the 1950s. In the 60s you were an artist first and foremost, and the best thing you could do was get a studio and work. How you then networked the art system—that phrase didn't even exist—was very, very social. It was how you might have been in with the newly formed Space studios or ACME—all sorts of things like that.

Untitled: stack; 2008

The Royal Festival Hall,
outside the Hayward Gallery,
Southbank, London
2008

Painted timber, plaster,
painted ply
Dimensions:
Stack 6m×2.5m;
Fence 3m×14m×9m

What has happened now is the wake-up call that an artist is just like everybody else—which they've always been in terms of financing their activity. But now it's just been thrown into complete highlight through Thatcherism and the whole assertion and emergence of an incredibly dynamic and successful art market. Whereas teaching, which was the great way of surviving as a practising artist, has gone into a decline. Art schools now find themselves as part of a divisive system where young artists, who might be fantastic contributing to art school life, don't want to go anywhere near it because of the commitment it requires.

You do have a lot of people in art schools who contend that world outside, but are becoming more and more isolated within academia. This is the last thing art schools need. An incredibly dynamic art world bubbling away, with artists making do and getting by with all sorts of different jobs, and then the art school being more and more drawn into an over-rationalised academic world with PhDs and endless accountability exercises, which are more like fault-finding exercises than anything constructive. All of which is absolutely fine, but the outside art world and the art school world are excluding each other more and more.

And I do know and feel that there is a very passionate generation of artists growing up now. They've been through so many deceits and cons politically. Not surprisingly, the one thing they can hold onto as something concrete is money. Not necessarily in a positive sense, but as a reality, a common denominator. Money has a crude reality about it.

Somehow that's reflected in the art system they're working within, the decisions they make about where to position themselves, and what kind of work they want to produce. There's pragmatism, ambition, desire and panic, all in equal doses, abounding in the emerging artist world, as well as amongst the not-so-emerging artists. We are all in it together, and hanging on to a romantic position can be a bit of a lost cause. But definitely worth a try.

Therefore, there isn't the need, or the time, or even the indulgence, to get in a great state of angst about sculpture or painting. It's like those things belong to a different political era. Perhaps they belong to the Cold War? Whereas now, there's something incredibly interesting going on, which is like a state of freefall.

How important is it to work within a gallery space? A surprising amount of your work has been shown in non-gallery spaces and outdoor venues, such as your recent work on the South Bank.

Incredibly important. And I would call a gallery space also some of those non-art spaces I've worked in, like a whole floor of a disused factory etc.

It's still a protected space. You still have to get your audience and bring them there, rather than your audience being a casual audience like at the South Bank or Canary Wharf, where the footfall is 10,000 people daily. So you have no idea who your audience is, and that's a very exciting prospect, although fraught with difficulties.

I don't like working out of doors. There's a freedom to not having walls. But again, the protected space, the art space is so fantastic. It is like a stage—that's where the relationship with theatre comes in—a space that can't be confused with anything else. The protected gallery space tells you you're going to look at art, so the ambition is for the art. Whereas, in a lot of places the ambition is for people—the people thing comes first. Now, there's nothing wrong with that, but it puts the art in this entertainment category.

The contemporary arts have experienced an explosion in popularity over the past couple of decades. But who or what has pushed the spectacle to the forefront—the artist, the audience, or the institution? There does seem to be an increasing aim for art to fulfil an entertainment role.

The synchronicity between Thatcherism taking hold, and a rising group of British artists in the late 1980s and early 90s, has had a sustained influence on the trajectory of art. Art became famous, successful, and financially significant. The institutions have embraced successful art wholeheartedly, and it has become linked with all sorts of unwelcome parasites: entertainment, people pleasing, constant economic justification, political correctness. Artists have lost control of their world, and their place in that world.

So artist, institution and audience have all colluded in the success of art, but not necessarily to the benefit of art itself. But the institutions have fallen for art as entertainment big time, and it's been one way for them to survive.

By playing on the theatrical or the spectacle?

I find that troubling. Penelope Curtis, director of the Henry Moore Institute, once said to me, 'Why is all your sculpture so big?' Because she's such a shrewd thinker, she then said, 'There's no such thing as a big sculpture. Because once you get to a certain point you're getting into the realm of competing with things that really are big.'

I'm not sure how I responded, but I know I see bigness as being about a relationship with making. Particularly the potential for making to go beyond my immediate control, to tempt a condition of being out of control. It's

Phyllida Barlow, New Sculpture,
Gallery and Grounds

New Art Centre,
Roche Court, Wiltshire
2007

Timber, felt, plywood, paint,
hardboard, plaster, cardboard,
cement, assorted fabrics
Dimensions: Variable

not to do with needing to make big sculpture as a given. It's actually to do with something like endurance—reaching beyond what is physically possible in terms of my height, stretch, etc. Also, recognising the processes of making as a performative act—extending beyond myself, emotionally as well as physically.

A bit like you might ask a mountaineer why on earth they climb that mountain, and they say, 'Because it's there'. And, for me, there's a very similar relationship with space and largeness, about my sense of being overwhelmed and whether it's possible to convey that to someone else. And that sense of being overwhelmed comes with all sorts of associations that are very different from the large spectacles of those Tate Modern Turbine Hall pieces. Different because those huge commissions lose intimacy, or theatricalise it so that the work has complete control over its audience that can seem almost totalitarian in spirit.

It's a pity that the spectacular and the huge can be negatively criticised as lacking intimacy and the personal. The intimate and the personal are exactly the things I want to claim for these large sweeps of stuff I use. And I hoped that at the BALTIC, by going up close to the tape surfaces, there would be that very close physical contact, as well as viewing and experiencing the big expanse of stuff from further away. And it's those qualities I want to explore again in the Mead Gallery. So the bigness isn't a showing off, it's a kind of testing out of an emotional weather system. Like seeing a vast storm cloud approaching, or seeing the expanse of a huge landscape.

I think the funding issues, and the money issues, and an increasing public awareness over the last 20 years that money and art go hand-in-hand, has been an enormous attraction in itself. This presents very, very obtuse problems in terms of what the experience actually is. For example, the fact that it's the Unilever Series at Tate Modern makes a huge difference to how that work is delivered. The last thing you feel the commissioning people want is something that's ephemeral at the point of delivery. They want that concrete experience to be there, and there's a sense of value for money being related to spectacle, size and inevitably, entertainment.

One of the myths surrounding your work is your reluctance to have anything to do with the commercial art world?

I'm having a whole change of mind about this. Also, I don't know if that is accurate. There's nothing wrong with selling work. I've never had a problem with that. I think we don't know how to resist capitalism—we're not equipped to do it. Where we've placed ourselves within an art world means we've signed up for capitalism whether we like it or not. If we want to disenfranchise ourselves from capitalism, I think it means an absolutely radical shift in so many ways, where art and life perhaps have to be absolutely entwined—where art and life are one and the same thing.

I want to think more about this, but I'm suggesting that to exist without any relationship to the art world demands making your art outside of it—and what does that mean, in reality, and what does that entail? Of course, it's possible. But the art world is voracious, and has the capacity to devour anything and everything. An 'outsider' becomes just as devourable as an 'insider'. Such is the success of this capitalist art world we're all having to live with.

I don't think about my work in relationship to any commercially driven incentives. It has to be about the urge to do it, first and foremost. And to reveal something, to be surprised, to let the work lead into uncharted waters, to let go. Not for selling to be the prime motive. However, fees and contracts for commissions etc. are becoming increasingly important. They are an economic incentive, very much so.

And in terms of exhibitions with gallery spaces, including museums—and the conditions which those institutions abide by—to me the fact is Gagosian puts on the best shows. Without any doubt whatsoever, the best way of seeing art in those places is to go to Gagosian. It's only playing one game, and it's absolutely clear about what that game is. The artist can deliver a certain level of work, in a certain state of completion. And a gallery of this calibre will expose the work ruthlessly. That's what the uncompromising, pristine space does. And it will sustain the viewer on its terms—on the unforgiving terms of the space and how the work stands up to that. It's a fantastic, beautiful brutality. Harsh, but also a reality check where the work has to survive the space.

Take the Serra, Giacometti, Fontana, Twombly show at Gagosian—you could actually go up to a Richard Serra, look at it and stand almost as though this thing was some wild beast about to unleash itself. You didn't have a silly little bit of wooden beading that you were going to trip over, like most public museums install. You could get absolutely within breathing distance of these extraordinary objects. And you can't do that anywhere else.

Therefore, there is something about where capitalism has succeeded within the visual arts that is very, very specific and quite exceptional. And, of course, Tate and all the museums are driven by capitalist forces. It's as much about the private use of capitalism as the public use of capitalism, how they compare, and how there are the same driving forces behind both. But the private realm can do things much more on their own terms much more, and when the space is fantastic, like Gagosian, the shows can be incredible. Therefore, we are in a very conflicted position. I don't think that's so much a complete loss of political integrity. It's an acknowledgement of a global economic climate.

You've described the process of Nightworks as part of your struggle to keep going, with a young family. Domesticity is a strong feature of your work, both in the circumstances of how it's made, and how it's presented and received.

This came up at this conference recently. There was a lot of post-feminist talk at this conference, and the whole feminist issue around having children, which just makes me cringe, because you have children and that's your responsibility. Then trying to be an artist as well is going to be complicated. But maybe family life just is complicated. And it was very difficult for about ten years.

For the Nightworks series you locked yourself away in the dark with the materials...

Yes, for a short time. For six months I was working like that. I wouldn't want to be known as the artist who made her work in the dark! It was a tremendous springboard to thinking about how to work very quickly, how to be very direct, how to explore sculpture, and how to make with no image in mind.

One of the problems with talking about Nightworks is that it becomes a story, another part of the Phyllida Barlow myth. I sense your resistance to this type of storytelling.

I went to do a talk at Goldsmith's in 1985, and I was describing for the first time, in front of a group of students, this process of making the work in the dark—because I'd got children and it was difficult, blah, blah, blah... It was a very cool audience. It was the Damien Hirst era. Suddenly, this voice from the audience said, 'What's more important to you, being an artist or being a mother?' And I had to say, 'Being a mother.' Because I think you can't deny that responsibility. That's the truth. And I remember this snigger, and then just this chill of, oh my God, this isn't holding water. And it was a really, really terrifying feeling. And I remember thinking, this is going to be a really long struggle to get the work seen, to get the work shown in the way that I'm framing it from a very domestic background, and a very domestic position.

Domesticity is a massive part of it, and a very private part of it. It's quite difficult to talk about, but very good to talk about it. My striving has been to industrialise the domestic. By going to builders merchants—the most masculine gendered spaces of all time—it's been something to do with the challenge of taking that hostility into the domestic environment.

The studio is right next door to the house, and when the children were small they were in and out of the studio the whole time. There wasn't a barrier, or I hope not. And it was difficult to get a run of time to make work. And in some ways it still is. That's because we're such a large family and there are a lot of conversations, issues, organising, plans and events that need to be discussed at any time of the day. The studio doesn't stop that. It's a constantly interrupted activity. And I think that automatically makes both the work and the studio itself somehow domestic.

But my ambition to make work is quite aggressive. Therefore, I've brought into that space a kind of masculine way of working—even if that's an incredibly simplistic way of describing it. It's to do with cutting and breaking, pulling and shoving. It's not to do with quiet activity—not that those aren't masculine. So the relationship with these materials, coming from expedient, functional places such as builders' merchants, sets a trend for what I'm trying to do in terms of challenging that domestic thing. But however much I challenge it, and seek out and reveal the darker side, it's still so rooted in the domestic in some way. It's painful acknowledging how dark the domestic can be.

What I find troublesome about the domestic element is that there's a certain audience within the art world which I now absolutely dread, because their reading of the work is so claustrophobically narrow. If the work is delivering a message that is sentimental and nostalgic, and I'm not interested in that message in that kind of way, then I think it's time to question something about that. It gives me the absolute creeps and really pulls me up by the bootstraps. It makes me realise that some of this language, and the intentions of the work, has got to explore its darker side. Because that's really what it is about.

As a teacher and artist you've been involved in developing the careers of many artists and watched some of those careers rocket over a short period of time.

It's wonderful to watch that, but it's like looking at the tribe across the valley—through the wrong end of the telescope. I've been talking to quite a few older artists of my age, or thereabouts, talking about this kind of thing, of being either locked into a particular trajectory, or, like myself, coming into something later, but with a long history of making behind one, and then seeing these extraordinary flourishing careers within five or six years of leaving art school, and for these instantly successful young, emerging artists there being no looking back.

But also, because I've been in it so long you see the demise of that, and the catastrophic effects. It's a huge landscape one is looking at of people who you think, good Lord, what's happened to them? They're no longer making art, they're doing something else. Or, poignantly, they are still making art—still at it, despite no longer being in the limelight.

It's such an unstable country. The ones who are still making extraordinary successful work, they will never not be that, because this is where the market is. The market needs to keep them there. It's like the stock exchange. However, recent events are throwing all these issues into a different context. Clearly, the stock exchange and the banks are unreliable in every respect. And so too is the art world.

What's been one of the biggest influences in your career?

Trying to sustain stability. That sounds really boring. Trying to make work and be very committed to the welfare of my children, my family. The last 30 years has been incredibly intense in that way. I haven't had any anxiety about success, but endless anxiety about how on earth do we juggle this? How do we, and how do I, bring in some kind of income for the making of the sculpture, because I want to keep that going, as well as support my family? And that's meant I've had to plod up the academic art-school ladder, which has been hard. Things haven't just happened click, click, click. It's been a slog in the art schools to get up that ladder. And with that has come huge responsibilities, which are so time consuming and quite pressurised. And I suppose I've had enough of that and I'm looking forward to leaving it.

The biggest influence has been trying to generate stability to work, and to be with the family, and to generate income. And it's been tough.

Previous pages:

STINT
—

Mead Gallery,
Warwick Arts Centre,
University of Warwick
2008

Timber, plywood, felt, paper,
cardboard, rubber, plaster,
concrete, tape, paint
Dimensions: Variable

BIOGRAPHY

PHYLLIDA BARLOW
Born Newcastle-upon-Tyne, 1944
Lives and works in London.

EDUCATION/AWARDS

1963
Chelsea College of Art Diploma,
Chelsea College of Art.

1966
Slade Diploma,
Slade School of Fine Art.

PROFESSIONAL HISTORY

1966-1967
Part-time Lecturer in Sculpture,
West of England College of Art.

1967-1978
Part-time Lecturer in Sculpture,
Chelsea College of Art.

1984-1986
Lecturer in Sculpture,
Brighton Polytechnic Fine Art Dept.

1986-1988
Lecturer in Sculpture,
Camberwell School of Art.

1988-1994
Lecturer in Sculpture,
Slade School of Fine Art.

1991-1993
Part-time Visiting Lecturer in
Sculpture, Chelsea College of Art.

1992-1994
Part-time Visiting Lecturer
in Sculpture, Royal College of Art.

1992
Acting Head of Sculpture,
Slade School of Fine Art.

1997-2004
Reader in Fine Art,
Head of Undergraduate Sculpture
Slade School of Fine Art.

2004-2007
Professor of Fine Art,
Director of Undergraduate Studies,
Undergraduate Tutor
Slade School of Fine Art.

2006
Joint Acting Head of School
with Professor John Hilliard,
Slade School of Fine Art.

2007-2008
Professor of Fine Art,
Slade School of Fine Art.

Director of Undergraduate Studies,
Undergraduate Tutor,
Slade School of Fine Art.

Head of Undergraduate Sculpture,
Slade School of Fine Art.

VISITING PROFESSORSHIPS

2006
Visiting Professor of Sculpture,
University of Lincoln Faculty of Art,
Design and Architecture.

VISITING ARTIST RESIDENCIES AND SEMINARS

2007
International Visiting Artists,
Programme, Umea University,
Visual Arts Dept. Sweden.

2006
Invited Lead Artist,
Bezalel Academy of Fine Art
and Design, Jerusalem, Israel.
Centenary event: exhibition critique
and panel discussion
'What is Art School For?'.

2004
Invited Lead Artist,
Poznan Academy of Arts, Poland:
Slade/Poznan collaboration.

2003
The McDermott Visiting Artist,
University of Texas at Dallas.

1996
Artist in Residence,
The International Art Education
Workshop, National College of
the Arts, Lahore, Pakistan.

1987
Artist in Residence,
Kettle's Yard, Cambridge University.

GOVERNORSHIP

1997-2001
Byam Shaw School of Art
Director/Chair of Governors:
Alister Warman.

SOLO EXHIBITIONS

2008
STINT, ten sculpture installation for Mead Gallery, Warwick Arts Centre, curated by Ronnie Simpson.

stack, fence, New Commissions for Southbank Centre.

Untitled, two sculpture commission for the Kilkenny Arts Festival, Ireland.

2007
Untitled: ramp, tower, flags 2007, Galeria Jesus Gallardo, Leon, Mexico.

Underover, nine sculpture installation commission, Canary Wharf, London.

New Sculpture: in the Gallery and Grounds, New Art Centre, Roche Court, Salisbury.

2005
Untitled: demo, nine sculpture installation, Studio 1.1, London.

A Sense of Place: A Place of Sense, 'Untitled: after', nine sculpture installation: Beacon Art Project, The Maltings, Sleaford, Lincs.

Remnants, Dallas, 2003, an exhibition of small sculptures by Phyllida Barlow, McDermott Visiting Artist, 2003, MAC, Centre for Contemporary Art, Dallas, Texas.

SCAPE, nine sculpture installation, Spacex, Exeter.

SKIT, seven sculpture installation, Bloomberg Space, London.

2004
Peninsula, nine sculpture commission, BALTIC, Centre for Contemporary Art, Gateshead.

Tannery Arts Exhibitions 2004, 'Phyllida Barlow', selected by Clem Crosby, Tannery Arts, Brunswick Wharf, London.

An installation and a selection of drawings to celebrate the publication of 'Objects for...and Other Things', Program, London.

Explicit Faith, four sculpture installation, choreographed by Gaby Agis, performed by Gaby Agis, Jo Moran, Florence Peake, Eva Mari Mukta, Marie Clair McKenna at The Jerwood Hall, St Lukes Church.

2003
Untitled: Dallas, 2003, five sculpture installation for the University of Texas at Dallas, Visual Arts Gallery, sponsored by the McDermott Foundation.

Remnants, 16 sculptures, curated by Nash Flores, The Magnet School, Dallas, Texas.

Remnants, 15 sculptures for the Angstrom Gallery, Dallas, Texas.

2002
New Sculpture, curated by Sotiris Kyriacou for the Richard Salmon Gallery, London.

Fete, installation curated by Louise Short for Station, Phoenix Wharf, Bristol.

2001
Knives in Hens, set design commissioned by The Attic Theatre Company, at Wimbledon Theatre, directed by Jenny Lee, written by David Harrower, touring to 11 venues throughout the UK.

GROUP EXHIBITIONS

2008
Stuff, with Alison Wilding, Laura White, Bettina Buck for V22 at Wharfe Road, London.

Prospects and Interiors Sculptors, drawings of 'Inner Space', curated by Sophie Raikes, Henry Moore Institute, Leeds. Accompanying essay by Sophie Raikes. ISBN9781905462223

STEW, curated by Andrew Stahl, Art Space Gallery, Michael Richardson Contemporary Art, London.

Entre Muros (Between Walls), curated by Reynaldo Thompson, CAS Gallery, University of Miami, Florida.

2007
etc..., curated by Sotiris Kyriacou, Amagerfaelledvej Art Project, Copenhagen.

says the junk in the yard, Flowers East, London.

An Exploration into Abstract Painting, Studio 1.1 Gallery, London.

3things, RUN, 24, an exhibition made by Donald Smith, Tudor Grove, London.

Art 38 Basel, New Art Center, Hall 2, stand W4, Messe Basel, the Swiss Exhibition Centre, Basel.

Rummage: Sculptors' Drawings, selected by John Gibbons, Winchester Gallery, Winchester.

Jumbo Shrimp, Woburn Slade Research Centre, curated by Theresa Liang and William West.

Entre Muros (Between Walls), Galeria Casa de los Manos, Leon, Mexico.

2006
Ebb and Flow, RAID Projects, Los Angeles.

Entre Muros (Between Walls), curated by Reynaldo Thompson, University of Guanajuarto, The Tomas Chavez Morado Gallery and Atrium; touring to Southside, Dallas, Texas, 22 artists from the Southside Artists In Residence Programme, University of Texas, Dallas.

Beauty and the Beast, selected and curated by Laura White and Richard Livingstone, Fieldgate Gallery, London.

Wandering Star, curated by Jeremy Akerman, GANA Art Centre, Seoul, Korea.

Royal Academy of Art Summer Exhibition, courtyard commission.

Please Close the Gate, Painted Sculpture at Roche Court, selected by Penelope Curtis.

2005
Sleigh, Arts & Business, London.

Zoo Art Fair, Studio 1.1, London Zoo, Mappin Terraces, London.

New Acquisitions: Works on Paper, Phyllida Barlow, Cecile Johnson-Soliz, Sarah Staton, Henry Moore Institute, Leeds.

Rough Diamond, Program, London

Drawing Two Hundred, Biennial Fundraiser, The Drawing Room, Tannery Arts, London.

Merveilles du Monde, Musée de L'Art Contemporain, Dunkirk, France.

Arte Fiera Bologna, Bologna, Italy.

Ebb and Flow, Three Colts Gallery, London.

2004
Love Story, curated by Erica Winstone for the Danielle Arnaud Gallery, London.

Zoo Art Fair: Program, Mappin Terrace, Regents Park, (eight artists), London.

Zoo Art Fair, (eight artists) Studio 1.1 Gallery, Regents Park, London.

BirdHouse, (20 artists) 38 Mitchell Street, London.

2003
Shelf Life, '60 minutes', curated by Gill Ord, Studio 1.1, London.

Location, Location, Location, 'Holed up: red yellow green pink', curated by Robert Rush and James Baachi-Andeoli, Albury Arts, Potsford House, Guildford.

The Drawing Auction, 'Untitled: engraved acrylic', The Drawing Room, Laburnum Street, London.

The Greatest Show on Earth, 'untitled: metropole, 2003', curated by Peter Fillingham, Metropole Gallery, Folkestone.

2002
Harvey's Bodies, 'Untitled: red coil', Metropole Gallery, Folkestone.

Royal Academy Summer Exhibition, 'Neck', invited artist, curated by Alison Wilding, Royal Academy of Arts, London.

2001
Station to Station, Spacex 2, 'Four', curated by Louise Short, Exeter Maritime Museum, Exeter, Devon.

Mile End Park Sculpture Exhibition, 'View', Mile End Park, Tower Hamlets, London.

British Art Show 5, 'After dark into black', commissioned by the Hayward Gallery, selected by Pippa Coles, Matthew Higgs, Jaqueline Poncelet, a National Touring Exhibition, organised by the Hayward Gallery, London. Supported by the Arts Council of England, 2000. Touring to Edinburgh, Southampton, Cardiff, Birmingham.

1999
Sculpture, 'Dawn till dusk', six sculptors, selected by Alison Wilding and John Maine, for the Triennial Sculpture Exhibition. The Royal Western Academy, Bristol.

O Pas La—Surprising Places, 'Far Away', L.A.C.: Lieu D'Art Contemporain, Narbonne, France, curated by Aude Herail Jaeger. Supported by the Henry Moore Foundation, FRAC, DRAC: Rousillon-Langueadoc, British Academy, British Council, Richard Salmon Gallery, James Herrick.

Furniture, 'Object for a Piano', curated by Paul Heber-Percy for Richard Salmon Gallery, London, touring to John Hansard Gallery, Southampton, Bluecoat Gallery, Liverpool.

Dumbfounded, 'Plug it, Bad fit, Stand up', curated by Carmel Buckley, Battersea Arts Centre, London, touring to New York, Chicago, San Francisco: 2001-2002.

1998
Not Nothing Nowhere, 'after dark', curated by Willy Robertson and Chris Mazieka, supported by Greenwich Millennium Fund, Docklands Millennium Regeneration, and private sponsors. The Master Shipwrights House, Deptford, London.

Out of Place, 'Time and Time Again', curated by Nilofar Akmut, from the National College of Arts, Lahore, Pakistan, International Workshop, supported by the Arts Council of Wales, Pakistan Airlines. Chapter Art Gallery, Cardiff, Wales.

Touching Matters, 'Little Drunks', commissioned by Camden Arts, The Gallery, Swiss Cottage Library, London, curated by Francois Dupre for the Women in Focus

The Ugly Edge, 'Big Bad Ugly', curated by Elizabeth Rosser, for the Ugly Edge Conference. The Henry Moore Institute Gallery, Leeds.

1997
EAST International, 'Truce', selected by Nicholas Logsdail and Tacita Dean, supported by the Arts Council of England. Norwich School of Art, Norwich.

PRIVATE COLLECTIONS

2007
'Untitled rack: timber, plaster, paint', Tate purchase.

2006
Seven drawings from 1970s-1990s, The Henry Moore Institute, Leeds.

'Untitled: yellow 2006', private collection.

Eight coloured drawings from 'Street Objects archive' 2001-2002, the Henry Moore Institute, Leeds.

APPOINTMENTS TO SELECTION PANELS AND AWARD PANELS

2008
Paul Hamlyn Award judge.

Red Mansion Prize judge.

Jerwood Sculpture Prize judge.

Curating Fellowship,
'Modern Times', Kettle's Yard,
Cambridge funded by the
Isaac Newton Foundation.

2007
Panel Judge for the Dupree
Family Award to a Woman Artist,
Royal Academy.

Judge for the Mark Tanner Sculpture
Prize at Standpoint Gallery.

2003
Invited nominator for the
Beck's Futures Arts Awards, ICA.

2001
Nominator for the Arts
Foundation Awards.

Nominator for the
Paul Hamlyn Award.

Selector for 'Sculpture',
New Ashgate Gallery,
Farnham, Surrey.

2000
Elected to the selection panel
for the new Slade Professorship.

1999
Selector for the Kettles Yard Open
Exhibition, Cambridge.

1998
Selector for the 1998
New Contemporaries, with
Eddie Berg, Christine Hohenbuchler
and Adrian Searle.
Chair: Sacha Craddock.

1995
Nominator for the Sculpture
Awards: The Arts Foundation,
(Nominator of Award Winner:
Melanie Counsell).

1994
Selector for the Prudential Awards
for the Visual Arts, with Cedric Price,
Richard Wentworth, chaired by
Julian Forrester.

1994-1998
Selection Panel: British School
at Rome, Fine Art Faculty Board.

1993-1994
Selection Panel: British School
at Rome, The Sargent Fellowship.

1990-1993
Selection Panel: The British School
at Rome, Rome Scholarship.

EDITORIAL BOARDS

2006
Sculpture Journal, editor Katherine
Eustace, published by Liverpool
University Press and the
Public Monuments Sculpture
and Monuments Association.

PRIZES, AWARDS

2007
£35,000 Award to an Individual
Artist, Arts Council of England.

2007
£45,000 Award to an Individual
Artist, Paul Hamlyn Foundation.

2006
£3000 The Dupree Family
Award to a Woman Artist,
Royal Academy of Arts.

GRANTS

2003
The Henry Moore Foundation
£5000 to Black Dog Publishing Ltd.
for production costs, including a
round-table discussion titled
Sculpture Now, for the monograph
'Objects for...and Other Things' on
the sculpture, drawings and writings
of Phyllida Barlow.

2003
The Elephant Trust,
£5000 for production costs of
'Objects for...and Other Things'
a monograph on the sculpture,
drawings and writings of Phyllida
Barlow, published by Black Dog
Publishing Ltd.

Dean's Award,
University College London.
Research travel award to the
University of Texas at Dallas, USA.

1996
Dean's Award,
University College London.

Research travel award to travel
to Lahore, Pakistan: International
Art Education Workshop, National
College of Arts.

1996
British Council Travel Bursary,
to participate in the International
Art Education Workshop at the
invitation of the National College
of Arts, Lahore, Pakistan.

1995
Elephant Trust Award, for a four-
sculpture installation, 'Depot', for
the Museum of Installation, London.

GALLERY TALKS AND LECTURES BY PHYLLIDA BARLOW GIVEN AT HER EXHIBITIONS

2007
Adapted version of Painting
Sculpture into a Corner, at the
University of Guanajarto, Mexico,
with reference to her exhibition
'untitled: flags, ramp, tower',
Galeria Jesus Gallardo, Leon, Mexico.

Phyllida Barlow; New sculpture
at Roche Court, a lecture and
discussion organised for local sixth
form colleges.

2005
Phyllida Barlow, Lucy Reynolds and
Tom Trevor in pre-exhibition
opening discussion, with reference
to her exhibition 'SCAPE' at
Spacex, Exeter.

Phyllida Barlow in conversation
with Sacha Craddock, curated
by J.J. Charlesworth at the
Great Eastern Hotel, for the internet
magazine E-digest edited by
J.J. Charlesworth.

2005
Phyllida Barlow in conversation
with Mark Godfrey, with reference
to her exhibition 'SKIT' at
Bloomberg Space.

2005
A Sculpture Workshop and Lecture
for A/As Level students with
reference to 'Peninsula', at BALTIC,
Centre for Contemporary Art,
Gateshead.

2004
Phyllida Barlow in conversation
with Sacha Craddock, in relationship
to her exhibition 'Peninsula',
BALTIC, Centre for Contemporary
Art, Gateshead.

2003
Aspects of Sculpture:
Three Lectures, 'Big Bad Ugly',
'The Sneeze of Louise' and 'Hearsay
Rumours, Bed-sit Dreamers and
Art Begins Today', with reference to
her exhibition 'Untitled: Dallas, 2003'
University of Texas, Dallas.

GALLERY TALKS & LECTURES: BY PHYLLIDA BARLOW IN RELATION TO OTHER ARTISTS' EXHIBITIONS

2008
Psycho Buildings, Hayward Gallery exhibition with 'stack, fence', Southbank Commission by Phyllida Barlow, gallery talk and discussion titled 'Public art: or not'.

2006
IMF Gallery, with Peter Suchin, Talk and Discussion for 'Get It Right', exhibition by Alex Costello.

2004
Contemporary Sculpture and the Work of Eva Rothschild, slide illustrated lecture, adapted version of 'Hearsay, Rumours, Bed Sit dreamers and Art begins Today', Zurich Kunsthalle, Switzerland.

2003
Lost for Words, slide illustrated talk on the work of Eva Hesse, MFA Seminar Programme, University of Texas, Dallas.

2003
Maelstrom, exhibition by Eric Prenelle Gallery, panel discussion and talk, 'The Ghost in the Machine'.

2000
Spectacular Bodies, the History of Art and Science from Leonardo to the Present Day, gallery debate with Professor Michael Baum, Emeritus Professor in Surgery, and Visiting Professor in Medical Ethics, UCL, and Phyllida Barlow. Hayward Gallery, London.

2000
Panamarenko, Tuesday Gallery Talk, Hayward Gallery, London.

1998
Pistoletto Retrospective, gallery talk, Museum of Modern Art, Oxford.

The Sneeze of Louise, Newcastle University Fine Art Dept. Artists' Lectures Series.

Playing with Paradox, opening talk 'Touching the Past' for the retrospective of the work of George Fullard, Kettles Yard, Cambridge and Mappin Art Gallery, Sheffield.

Louise Bourgeois: New Work, gallery talk, Serpentine Gallery, London.

Out of Place, gallery talk for the visually impaired, Chapter Art Gallery, Cardiff.

Rose Finn Kelcey: New Work, joint gallery talk and discussion, Phyllida Barlow and Guy Brett, Camden Arts Centre, London.

Tony Cragg: New Work, Paper Tiger, gallery talk, Whitechapel Art Gallery, London.

1997
The Sneeze of Louise, organised by Alison Sleeman, History of Art Department: Sculpture Seminars, University College, London.

1996
TRY, exhibition 'Sculpture-Dead or Alive', gallery talk and discussion, Royal College of Art, London.

The Sculpture of Louise Bourgeois, 'The Sneeze of Louise', gallery talk for the Friday Review at Oriel Gallery (Arts Council of Wales), Cardiff.

The Hatred of the Object, University of Essex Art History Dept., in collaboration with the Cambridge Darkroom Gallery.

1995
The Rites Of Passage, exhibition, 'The Sneeze of Louise: the Sculpture of Louise Bourgeois', Tate Gallery, London.

1993
The Sculpture of Susana Salano, gallery talk, Whitechapel Art Gallery, London.

1991
Pistoletto—a Retrospective, gallery talk, Camden Arts Centre, London.

1990
For the 'Sightlines Gallery Talk' series on the installation exhibition Seven Obsessions at Whitechapel Art Gallery, London.

CONFERENCE PAPERS AND PANELS

2008
What is the Future of Art Education?, panel discussion member for the Art Monthly series on art education, with Pavel Buchler, Vaughan Grilles, Michael Corris, chaired by Patricia Bickers.

The Subjective Objective, a symposium co-ordinated and chaired by artist in residence Kate Davis, Cove Park International Art Centre, Rosneath, Argyll, Scotland, talk by Phyllida Barlow.

2007
TRADE: Artists in Conversation, Phyllida Barlow, Alfedo Jarr, Patricia C. Phillips, Leitrim and Roscommon Visual Arts Programme Seminar and Residency, Boyle, Roscommon, Eire.

How to Make, (or Artist as Hostage), a response to Bresson's A Man Escaped, post screening talk, at PEER for Canal on Viner Street curated by Gareth Jones.

2006
The Language of Art, curated by Joe Moran, Chisenhale Dance Space Workshop Events.

What Will You do with That Degree?, panel discussion with Andrew Renton, Professor Sam Ainsley. Ben Gurion Airport. The Centenary Events for Bezalel, Jerusalem, Israel.

Interdisciplinary Forum, co-ordinated by Jon Houlding, Royal College of Art, London.

2005
Permission to Fail, talk and seminar, co-ordinated by Abigail Reynolds, Ruskin School of Drawing, Oxford University, Oxford.

Research Spaces, Materialisation of Practice in Art and Architecture, 'Transitional Spaces: Phyllida Barlow, Ship in a Bottle', an illustrated talk by Phyllida Barlow on her work—Slade/Bartlett conference, Woburn Research Centre, University College London.

2004
Treason of Images: Teaching Modern Art, installation session, chaired by Helen Charman, 'Throwing Away the Maps', slide illustrated talk by Phyllida Barlow. Tate Modern, London.

The Artist Educator:
Entrepreneur or Educator?,
chair of panel discussion, 'Liberation,
Responsibilities and Being at Home',
with Richard Wentworth,
Mark Wallinger and Eva Rothschild,
Tate Britain, London.

2003
Barnet Newman Study Day,
Tate Modern/Open University,
coordinated by Sophie Howarth and
Gill Perry. Edited version of 'Hearsay,
Rumours, Bedsit Dreamers and Art
Begins Today', Tate Modern, London.

2002
Eva Hesse Symposium,
'Encountering Eva Hesse',
Tate Modern/Leeds University
collaboration coordinated by
Professor Griselda Pollack:
'Lost for Words', slide illustrated
talk on the work of Eva Hesse,
Tate Modern, London.

The Whitechapel Art Gallery
Seminar Series: Next Generations,
Current Sculptural Practice in the
UK and Beyond, 'Hearsay, Rumours,
Bed-sit Dreamers, and Art Begins
Today', slide illustrated talk by
Phyllida Barlow, in conjunction with
the exhibition 'Early One Morning'
and with Iwona Blazwick,
J.J. Charlesworth, and Niru Ratnam,
Whitechapel Art Gallery, London.

Royal Academy of Arts: Architecture
Forums, The City as Sculpture:
From Skyline to Plinth, 'In and Out
of the City', a slide illustrated talk
for a panel discussion chaired by
Richard Cork, with Antony Gormley,
Royal Academy of Arts, London.

2001
NYU in London: Saturday Artists
Seminar, 'What is Public Art?',
'Big Bad Ugly' slide talk.

Studio Lives: Contemporary Views
by Artists, slide talk by Phyllida
Barlow on her work and its
relationship to the studio.
Henry Moore Institute, Leeds.

Selector's event, New
Contemporaries: panel discussion
with Eddie Berg, Jennifer Higgie,
at the Camden Arts Centre, London.

Southern Arts Board, conference,
Artistic Judgements: a discussion
about quality in the visual arts, at
St. Catherine's College, Oxford.
Report with paper titled 'On Being
Judged', Les Buckingham (ed.),
published by Southern Arts April,
2001, pp.3-10.

**VISITING ARTISTS'
LECTURE PROGRAMMES:
Illustrated Talks given by
Phyllida Barlow on her work,
and her work in relationship
to other artists.**

2008
Making It Up, for Sheffield
University Visual Arts Department
'Transmissions' Lecture Series and
Forum, curated by Sharon Kivland
and Carl Von Weiler.

Making It Up, Cardiff Institute
of Visual Arts and Design Visiting
Artists Lecture Series, co-ordinated
by Cecile Johnson-Soliz.

2007
Making it Up, International
Artists Lecture Programme,
Umea University Visual Arts
Department, Sweden.

Painting Sculpture Into a Corner,
Academy of Fine Arts, Copenhagen.

2006
Inaugural Lecture, appointment to
Professor of Fine Art, Painting
Sculpture into a Corner, J.Z. Young
Lecture Theatre, UCL.

Painting Sculpture into a Corner,
Ferens Fine Art Lecture Series,
Hull University.

2005
Painting Sculpture into a Corner,
illustrated lecture on the work of
Phyllida Barlow, lecture series
organized and selected by Pavel
Buchler, Cornerhouse Fine Art
Lecture Series.

Phyllida Barlow: Artists' Talks,
Programme, Goldsmiths BA Fine Art.

2004
Visiting Artist-in-Residence Lecture
Programme, Poznan Academy of
Arts at Skoki, Poland.

2003
Phyllida Barlow: Big Bad Ugly,
University of Texas at Dallas, Texas.

Phyllida Barlow: Big Bad Ugly,
Southside on Lamar, Dallas, Texas.

2002
Phyllida Barlow: Recent Work,
Newcastle MA Fine Art Course.

2001
Phyllida Barlow: On the Edge,
Newcastle University MA Fine Art
Seminar Slide Talk.

Phyllida Barlow: On the Edge,
Visiting Artists' Lecture Programme
and Seminar, Cardiff Institute of
Art and Design, Cardiff

PUBLICATIONS

2008
HOST, for Sheffield Hallam
Transmission lecture series,
transcribed by Carl Von Weiler,
Arts Wordspress.
ISBN 9781906441142

2007
How to Make, or Artist as Hostage:
A view of Robert Bresson's 'A Man
Escaped', (Un Homme Condamné
à Mort s'est Échappé'),
Lilly Plender (ed.), Untitled, July 2007.

'Carl Plackman Sculpture Drawing
Writing' catalogue for Beyond
Appearances the Sculpture of
Carl Plackman, 1943-2004,
Huddersfield Art Gallery, text by
Phyllida Barlow.

Remembering Carl Plackman,
Jon Wood (ed.), Huddersfield Art
Gallery, p37. ISBN 9780900746901

Sean Edwards, catalogue text
for www.chapter.org

2006
Encountering Eva Hesse,
Griselda Pollack and Vanessa Corby
(ed.), from the Tate Modern
conference, 'Encoutering Eva Hesse'
co-ordinated by CATH, Leeds
University, lecture titled
'Lost for Words', London, Germany,
US: Prestel, 2006, pp.217-221.
ISBN3-7913-3309-7

2005
Helsinki Photography Festival,
'to be continued...Making Time',
catalogue text for British Council
touring exhibition on Gary Stevens'
performance work, Finland:
Valokuvagalleria Hippolite and
British Council.
ISBN0-8635-5548-9 (UK)

2003
Testing for Lies, in exhibition
catalogue, 'Edward Fellows:
Drawings and Photographs',
Rushy House, Brixton, London.

A Severe Weather Warning,
in 'BAG', Melanie Counsell exhibition
catalogue, Jaques Fournel (ed.),
Sete, France: Editions Ville Saint
Clair, Aug. 2003. pp.58-59.

Picture, film still from 'Mandy' (1952)
with text, Frieze magazine, issue 74,
UK: Durian Publications Ltd. April
2003, pp.53-4. ISSN 09620672

2002
Angela de la Cruz: Notes from a
studio visit, 22 July 2002.

...From the Mouth to the Tail,
Slade Magazine, Slade Publications,
Aliki Braine (co-ed.), 2002, pp.1-2.

The Royal Academy Forum,
The City as Sculpture: from the
plinth to the sky', 'In and Out of the
City', The Architectural Review,
pp.90-1, June 2002. ISSN0003-861X

The Sculptor Speaks, a response
to the conference on the HMI's
collaboration with the National
Sound Archive production of an oral
archive of sculptor's voices. The
Henry Moore Institute Newsletter,
Liz Aston (ed.), Much Hadham, UK:
The Henry Moore Foundation, p.2,
February 2002. ISSN1363-1152

PUBLICATIONS ON THE WORK OF PHYLLIDA BARLOW

2006

Phyllida Barlow: Teacher and
Student, interview by Mark Godfrey
for Frieze, Art Schools.

Then and Now,
101, September 2006 pp.168-75.
ISSN 0962 0672

2005

Sense of place; place of sense,
Beacon Art Project, John Plowman
and Sally O'Reilly, Beacon,
Lincolnshire. ISBN1860502032

UTDallas Southside, The first two
years, Richard Brettell and
Karen Weiner (ed.), Dallas: University
of Texas Press.

Phyllida Barlow: Peninsula,
exhibition catalogue to accompany
nine sculptures commissioned
for the 4th floor gallery of BALTIC,
Centre for Contemporary Art,
Gateshead, BALTIC.
ISBN1-903655-22-6

2004

Objects for...and Other Things,
Duncan McCorquadale (ed.),
a monograph on the sculpture,
drawings and writings of
Phyllida Barlow with texts by
Mark Godfrey and Jon Wood,
transcribed round table discussion,
'Sculpture Now', chaired by
Phyllida Barlow with Richard
Deacon, Charles Harrison, and
others, London, New York:
Black Dog Publishing Ltd. 288pp.
ISBN 1901033597

TV/RADIO APPEARANCES

2008

'What is the future of art education',
live debate from Ikon Gallery,
Resonance FM radio station.

2007

CNN profile on Rachel Whiteread,
produced by Pamela Borovsky.

2005

'Art School', BBC2, 1-10 September,
final critical session with
Sacha Craddock, Richard Cork,
J.J. Charlesworth, and others,
Endemol Television Productions,
Bristol, presented by Claudia
Winkleman, filmed at Chelsea
College of Art, Millbank, University
of the Arts, London.

THANK YOU

Phyllida Barlow would like to thank Ronnie Simpson for his support and enthusiasm during the making and installation of STINT. The exciting and challenging opportunity to produce the works which constitute STINT, and which were produced specifically for the Mead Gallery space, was greatly facilitated by his understanding and knowledge of artists' diverse and different creative activities. He has been keen to respond to the ambitions of the work, and it has been an important experience producing the work in the studio and installing it in situ.

Phyllida would like to extend further thanks to David Garnett for his invaluable knowledge, innovative skills and expertise, his swift ability to troubleshoot technical problems and his efficiency in liaising between the production of the work, its transportation and its installation.

Also, and importantly, the following studio assistants are to be thanked, warmly and with great appreciation, for their endurance, tolerance, insightful comments, humour, critical stimulation, exasperation and, above all, hard work and resilience. It has been a great bonus working with them:

Mark Davey
Laura Emsley
Nick Mortimer
Lewis Peake
Steve Shiell
Charlie Yetton

Also, Phyllida would like to thank the technical crew at the Mead Gallery for their tireless contributions in the installation of the work:

Tom, Brian, Michael, Becky and Irene.

These thanks and appreciation would not be complete without mentioning Phyllida's husband Fabian, and all her children and their partners:

Flos and Des, Clover and Mark, Tabby and Harry, and Eddie and Lewis.

Thanks to all and everyone who, throughout August and September 2008, has been involved in one way or another in the production of STINT.

Last but not least, Phyllida extends her appreciation and gratitude to Stefi Orazi for the design and production of the catalogue for STINT. It has been a pleasure working with her.